Memory and the Call of Waters

(Poetry)

S. Su'eddie Vershima Agema

Winner, Association of Nigerian Authors Prize for Poetry 2014

Nominee, Wole Soyinka Prize for Literature 2018

ISBN: 978-978-54899-4-1

http://sevhage.wordpress.com
SEVHAGE
Black Gate Trove, No 3, MFM Street, Karu, Nasarawa State

sevhage@gmail.com
Makurdi. Karu. Abuja. Ibadan.
Brighton (United Kingdom)
+234 (0)703 028 5995; +234 (0)807 358 0365.

Cover Picture: Patrick Akam for Vzoren Photography
Cover Concept and Design: S. V. Agema and Gabriel B. I. Agema
Book Design: Su'eddie V. Agema
Editors: Innocence Silas, Aôndosoo Labe, and Oko Owoicho

Praise for S. Su'eddie Vershima Agema's Poetry

'Su'eddie's poetry is precociously profound. There aren't many poets of this generation whose art possess such depth of themes; such sophistication of diction' —**Reward Nsirim**, author of *Fresh Air and other Stories*

"These are deep words from a deep mind reflecting on the deep things of life. The reflective musings of this young poet portend a promising rich future" —**Maria Ajima**, *Multiple award-winning writer and scholar.*

'Su'eddie makes the writing of modern poetry as easy as drinking a glass of water. It is a supreme act of imagination and intelligence, the restoration of lost stories...' —**Joshua Agbo**, literary scholar and dramatist.

"Su'eddie's poems like songs serenade the core of anguish and at the same time tease the ease of our most mellow moments... His is a rare talent" – **Unoma Azuah**, *Multiple award-winning writer and scholar*.

'Agema's message(s) is profound, far-reaching; his anecdotes and allegories are mind-blowing and instructive. His social responsiveness and commitment to this end is palpable and can by no means be over-emphasised. The poet understands unmistakably that poetry vis-à-vis literature is the nexus that transforms and mitigates the social morass in which man has sadly found himself.' —**Emma Inedu**, literary scholar, poet and author, *Cockcrow at Noon*.

Is it possible for poetry, *real* poetry, to be written on the back of a postage stamp? My answer is 'YES', and my example – Su'eddie Vershima Agema. And where such poetry is interspersed with much longer ones and threaded into a common universe of themes with them, the overall effect is simply enthralling. —**Hyginus Ekwuazi**, multiple award-winning poet and literary scholar.

Agema's lyricism is a bold and beautiful delight. A rich talent that continues to push the boundaries of what poetry can be. – **Servio Gbadamosi**, Poet and Winner of the 2015 Association of Nigerian Authors' Prize for Poetry.

This book is specially dedicated to:
The people of Mbalom, Frs Joseph Gor, Felix Tyolaha & Solomon
Mfa Ukeyima
Also, for Agatha and Msen, Chris and Gabriel, Hyginus Ekwuazi,
Jennifer, Nathaniel, Theo, & all my siblings.
May memory be mild, and the times treat us kind.

CONTENTS

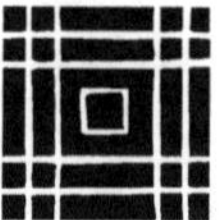

Before Learning a New Normal

The annals of history are replicated in deep pains
painting permanent pictures that cling to my heart's canvas.

I live on as the sun dives to its bed drowning memories
of bastard frauds who offered salvation to suffering saints
who kiss rings, genuflect and worship doctrines
mixed to local sanctification of stomachs and loins.

Outside, the people see a white collar around my neck.
How many know the tale of my soul, burned
by superiors who poked away religion from my hold
as forced thrusts gave me the right of passage to perform rites
of forgiveness for many sins not near in weight to mine?

I hear the voice above the waters and see a dove descending
not after baptism but after my several murders:
This is my beloved ape in whom I am well pleased

I save Gaea as I cleanse the land of the filth of a lot growing fat on fear
(May I be spared any blood that might call from the earth—
maybe these Cains would wear the cloak of Abel in death)
and let Oshun drink her fill as she watches these clerks of the devil
find their way to Hades or what eternity reserves for them.

Slowly, the waters lose the sparkles of red on their stomach
replaced with a silver lamp surrounded by a million candles.
From far-off woods, owls hoot as white demons ring bells…

I am a spirit.

Humanity hangs upon my being, flesh. I look to the skies, but the view is a stranger to my eyes. The constellations I grew up in are hidden. A blanket has been drawn over heaven's vastness and the top view mirrors that which is aground. I fear. The heart of man has made the heavens hide its diamonds for fear of contamination that will rid them of their lustre. How will anyone know? They have built their constellations and lights shine from distance multi-eyed monsters looking down on minions. Babel has built its towers with the million tongues of men. They have conspired to fight the heavens and eat the weak. They have one voice, armed with passion and intent.

I am a spirit. Humanity hangs upon my being. I shall transform to the new tongue; spite and infest them with what madness I can. Never shall contentment rest upon their brows. Time will sing their song, but it will tune the destruction the future holds.

Ah. Heaven's lights twinkle again. It is time.

Learning a new normal

While nature slept, the devil fried the skies
Placed a pint of water to man's mouth
Farted what became polluted winds
Slapped the earth, then
Dropped one word
And a new normal was born.

The Genesis of Belief

Your first drop was the void formed before time
You, whose legs are the foundations of the skies
    whose eyes looked down on emptiness
before He created the chasm making your face a mirror
looking at itself; the heavens to the sea.

Pulled from your ways, I come again
to these million sparkles birthed by solar jewels dancing on your waves
I hold to their glamour
wondering at the darkness that lies hidden on your floors
knowing lunar sparkles will replace the deception of your depth.

II
I shall write my heart on your stomach
carving my pain in the fluid loss of your expanse
lost in the turning sheets that twist in many waves
knowing its flow will take my words
and the anger that falls upon the plain.

Let there be light II

(from a story most of us know quite well)

It was our Genesis
the beginning of a continuation
of our potentials' quick Exodus

Then every ruler shouted promises like the Lord
sparking our hopes as we heard their crackling voices rise:
       'Let there be light!'

Trust our Non-Existent Power Authority:
The darkness pervades our lives
wearing us gloom

The Problem Has Changed Name
corporation turned to a million DisCos
promising rebirth, dances and a beauty bloom

It was the twin of faux freedom
that gave us the power of grating noises
as we bark above generators or hiss at the dark

Indeed, we brew thunder and fart noises
which amount to zilch in our hydro-electric dreams
projecting our collective sustainable deterioration goals

A drunkard preaches the politician's book of Revelation:
a harvest will come of our dams
yea, we would surely reap several *Damns!*

ADDENDUM:
Gen 1:3 And God said '*Let there be Light*'
...NEPA[1] replied: '*Mba nu!*'

---

[1]National Electric Power Authority

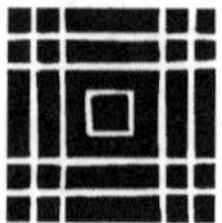

BUILDING MEMORIES AND SONGS

I am building memories, a song of waters from a hold on Mother's Day.
I get my memories caught in open doors and transition to a fallen house,
then flip the bird at the sun.

Building memories

I build memory
one block tenderly placed on another
of love and disaster; right steps and wrong songs
time cementing each with sorrows savoured, lessons learnt.

Slowly, materials disintegrate
s h a *t t e r* i n g what was once me.

The years *wither* to dust
and I am left to start building afresh
lost in the sands that have become my now.

A song of the waters

(for Niyi Osundare, after a mother's dream during Katrina)

Life gathers strings and tune to wailing winds singing
to spirits sailing at seas flowing from Ikere to Orleans.

Pain weaves a coat and wears your being
sending jabs across the miles. You shiver to the winds, stuck in time
as you hold on to a raft for life, your mother's voice rings:

Let the grey from the heart of this forest fly
through my dreams to your heart.
Hold, this star shall sing softly to the dance of life.

Drawn from this water's womb, you shall have many days
Days on end shall be a song without wrong placed on your tongue. It
shall spread in lines to ink hope beyond thoughts and seasons.

Not a thousand floods shall swallow your soul
time shall find you on your feet, conquering the many waters singing
to the lute of abundance, with dancers praising your worth.

Hold, the waters shall dry.
Hold, the waters shall bear you up.

Memory's hold on Mother's Day

(for Chris Ayede-Agema, Marie Aduro, Dora Oyana, Eugenia Abu & Agatha Agema)

The fires of life are lit from wombs
that warm nine months to bring wonders
whose brightness deny smokes.

Theirs are tales,
ours, all narratives—

these tales fill our life
footnotes of strife that mount memories,
foundations of our strength, to fight, win, lose and live.

II

An early chapter appears on my mind's sheets:
Me, shivering with upturned eyes
my tale spiralling to a close
even as I called your name to deliver me from fever
          Mummy!
What other name burns in a child's heart
in times of strain?

But you were far away,
seeking means to find our bread of sustenance.
You arrived home at midnight, after a seventeen-hour shift,
wearing tiredness like a coat.

Your eyes met my shivering frame.
Motherly instinct undressed your exhaustion,
as you picked me up
your feet became wings speeding our run
to the *nearest* hospital miles away.

We had silence for our companion
and when it became too comfortable
a sob from you or some more clattering from me
we found the home of healing after an eternity on our feet;
me on your back like a rider on a donkey.

By dawn, I was well enough to smile my way to another day,
you simply took your bath and found the road to work again

III

The chapters roll and quickly, I find myself
years away: our tale has made me a wandering man
seeking bread for *my* mouth
and the boy who took a ride on your back yesterday
walks the streets today to seek remnants of wealth
that hides in the country's yesterday.

Your voice is a whisper that sneaks on the other side,
a laugh only you can conjure appears in my mind
I try to translate it to words
but you cut me short:
> *hello son... I can't talk much... the boss is watching*
> *and I have hours to clock before I close...*

It is Sunday and your increasing grey is no excuse
to decrease your Manor hours, seeking
the bread you have placed on our tables
through the several pages of our tales.
I nearly charge at Napoleon who lets you work
blind to the bend time has brought to your waist...

The piper dictates, You answer my unsaid charge

I swallow poverty's impotence
the line clicks off as work drags your love away
leaving me with a memory of warmth no distance can hide

IV Epilogue
Aôndo, if you live above the clouds as you do in our hearts
best author writing our tales
please, rid her of every torment
send memory to help give her more pleasurable moments…

Let the spirit of every fire live on
let the smokes be dispersed…
Life is a narrative, and you, Mother, remain the heart of this tale
a fire that burns bright in all our hearts.

Memories caught in open doors

Memories walk into my dreams
I wake to find my thoughts asleep
Yesterday is a weight flung beyond reach

The Benue sings with the waves
I wiggle, watching fishers
locked in a dance of doubt

I clap at empty blasphemies
and heresies that replace the fire of forceful thrones,
dominions and deities, mermaids and ancestors

Celestial forces that lived in my heart—
blocked off behind doors I have fortified—
roam the boundaries of my sleep till I am forced awake

I jump at the sight of an open door.
Did fatigue force my heart shut, forgetting
a cycle of evil that sways slowly to the waltz of dawn?

A bird flies in through the door
a song escapes its throat as it hovers
then flies out through the open door.

Finding the road to your ends
(for Ify Omalicha and a few others)

Your nimble hands scribbled notes
and played a verse that called my heart
to a dance my feet tapped to.

Procrastination put iron shoes to a meeting
where both our smiles would have dined
while we sipped of shared bliss...

Slowly, I took off those shoes and found the road to your ends
but got news on arrival that you had found the road to my ends—
found the road on that journey to your eternal end...

They speak of you now in 'was' tenses:
"She WAS delivered by the roads to the summons
of Everyman."

Anguish boils in my soul
and sorrow becomes a flood
that breaks my eye banks in streams.

Can I find the ease to kiss away this sorrow
of words that never came
proclaiming my love of your verse and... *you?*

Transition

(for Hembasoon, Ernie, Verun, Charles Ayede, TV Agema, P. Aduro, Prof Ker, Prof Agada, Pius Adesanmi, Wilfred Bula & too many others)

The earth's hunger is eternal
its stomach swells with our loved ones

in farewell, we make concrete beds
and mound pillows

scribbles show senseless summaries
of names and dates while bodies rot within

these graves are an encyclopaedia
pages of our mostly forgotten past

Stars, Out

The stars went out and so did the moon.
The singer stopped playing and went to bed...
- Langston Hughes 'The Weary Blues'

The stars put out their lamps
Leaving the sky grey.
The moon compensating, smiled
A clear ball, different from yesterday's banana
We stayed an eternity with you
But just as our hearts counted a second
The night rolled its mat
Bringing in the reality of day.

When traffic lights go wrong

(For Pius Adesanmi and the 156 beautiful souls lost to the Ethiopian air crash. With very fond memories and a million pains)

I

An Ethiopian bird crashes
The symbol on her tail becomes the traffic lights gone wrong
In sharp ascension to a mighty descent:

Green, the fertile souls in her bowel. *Life goes on.*
Yellow, the agony of the final moments. *Pause.*
Red, a few minutes quickie with Thanatos at Gimbichu. *Stop.*

II

Death harvests 157 names from a hidden manifest
Tribes blame Anubis, Eshu, and the devil
A few pray for grace and ask that the heavens keep Hades away.
People watch screens and refresh tabs for news of a miracle.

Those who follow Odinani acknowledge
Ala has made a deal with Amadioha
The skies bow to the ground
And Chukwu watches his servants become ancestors.

While some sigh, certain hearts beat a definite bye
Biting fingers without hope
Listening as empty sympathies ring.

III

We send hugs to the kin of rumoured flighted souls
The manifest still hides in the shell of fearful airlines
Finally, the list comes to light, and we find our hearts crack

The rainbow becomes a worthless promise
Eyes stream floods on this pious dawn

As Ede notes, regrets step in.
Doves fly with olives, but we see the cloaked reaper shouting:
Armageddon! Armageddon!
This sickle is for you!

We seek hope in transcendence or a reincarnation
But the weight of love invested in lost vessels blot out faith
And becomes a sea of grief that drowns our tired hearts.

Transition II

Our compound is a testament to the earth's theft,
littered with concrete mounds, pillowed with
fading names. Forgotten stories.

There's this river behind the compound,
it whispers of time and waves when I arrive
telling tales of when herders kissed our cheeks.

On the water's brown belly, glittering to the sun's kiss
I see a reflection of an untamed bearded man
with wild eyes shutting from the weight of a thousand woes
different from the boy with wide eyes filled with the wisdom
of careless abandon and the weight of only adventure.
These eyes carry pain and the knowledge of an adult's strife.

This river, this river…running behind the houses,
rushes with urgency and waves as I leave,
warning of the time when herdsmen might lead us to Golgotha.
Our ityô, the elders stand helpless while my daughter sighs from afar.
I raise a dirge of too many memories filled with holes,
waiting to be patched when I become the earth.

The story of our streets today

Today, one generator and a TV
Were taken away from someone
Light and hope was stolen from that home
He lost his head and swore to get someone else's

Today, a man was caught
Who stole a generator and television
He was the thief of someone else's vision
Seeking means to fight Hades who called to his mother

Today, a mob roasted a man
With a generator and television
While his mother died waiting to get money
For drugs the chemist valued at a hundred bucks.

A house has fallen

A house has fallen
and a family scatters.
The blocks are used to build a city.

Where the house once stood
weed grows, thick.
A wall still stands there

On it is a picture,
a withering old woman.
Alone.

Flipping the bird at the sun

I look the sun in the eye
make to flip it the bird
then feel a plat on my head.

The sun smiles to say I should also do a trick
I shield my eyes from staring too long at it
and clean the bird poop from my head.

NOTES, EKO AND NOSTALGIA

We write our hearts in notes before sunset, thinking of Ibadan

We shiver, we lie heavy from the vanity of dreams—
the scholar's endless hope for grace.

Lenrie once asked *what it costs to be loved
and left alone?* We lose hope but keep an *eye open on the sea.*

Our seers flip cowries and bring promise, so we bid our time
turning the tide to a new verse, walking slowly—
birds tweet dawn.

Notes before sunset at Eko

The birds tweet as dawn lifts the curtains of day:
The sounds stir the soul, shifting troubles for a second
but depression soon finds her space at the centre
like the sun's gradual ascent to its throne
frying frustration in several servings till light finds darkness

Hemingway inspires on this road to perdition
Plath, Sexton, Sello Duiker and Berryman wave alternate routes:
We must travel in the direction of our fears
to beds where hugged pains would be forgotten;
Voices are drowned in mouthfuls of lasting silence.

Ibadan

The strokes on your children's faces are washed
By the flood of folks who continually call you mother
The remains of tradition are left in tongues that defy
Cosmopolitan hugs of visitors who come in from varied lands
You accept their hugs and lay mats for them to become your children
Despite the offspring of your womb who hold on to the irony
Of a love that welcomes and yet alienates.

Stomachs dance to sweaty black mountains with ewedu
Eyes feast on riveting rusty roofs, legs stretching to Jericho for books
Pilgrims trace the footprints of Mbari, the Black Orpheus and transitions
Carved in history as other steps find life in new genial sands.

I have tasted your goodness, and I am lost in your ancestral modernity
Looking from Broking House heights and Cocoa's cliffs, Dugbe's heart is
    shown in Mokola's madness
    a million souls strip off sanity for shame as they forage in nature's suit

Ibadan, your cemeteries swell, and Eko lures a trickling count
Yet, your stomach bloats with endless lines of ants who march
From Challenge to Samonda and beyond
Accidents await as automobiles kiss each other or eat raw flesh
Like your many other contraptions.

You hold out, patiently, Ibadan, gazing at your lands from Bower's top
For you know every water shall dry and memory will revere you.

If Lagos knew

(for Abulatan Wuraola)

If Lagos knew, its sounds would be a saner song
in the hearts of those whose tunes an orchestra never loses beat to.
The roads wouldn't rage with the anger of hustlers in BRTs, *kekes* and *danfos*
swearing, sweating in hope for a slice of the Island's promise.
It wouldn't grind all to its slow pace or halt time for folks, whose foreheads
fold into waves of worries as adrenaline increases several thoughts
raised from internal pain as they try to escape the sun's whip
lucky folks shielded in moving tents filled with gases that purr noiselessly
bringing the harmattan to closed chambers on another hot noon…

If Lagos knew, even if the chaos were gathering from Ajegunle to Ikotun
or overt poshness descending from the Island to Maryland
there would be that pause for the wind to dance across the skies
leaving imprints of colours and shapes in cones and candles
for the waves to dance across the waters in claps and hurrahs
for the beautiful tapestry seen from Third Mainland to be rearranged:
and that beauty captured by several lenses to be seen in a new light,
the sun kissing her belly in a million sparkles, those boats in proper
    formation.

If Lagos knew, it would change, if only for one moment
to breath in deep, of this nativity
Bethlehem slept but Lagos hustles on another sunny day.
And as another placenta gets buried
Eko's beauty is crafted in the sound of another infant cry.

When walks turn to dares after Greek legends

I
The night is a demanding force that pushes darkness into many souls
I go through the day, hugging the sun, but emptiness eats me at dusk
even when false lights shine from above.

I am trapped in a waiting room in purgatory.
When will I see the moon shine from my window—
see my wife sleeping and kiss my child?

Brighton never sleeps, and in vain, I stare at night skies
where the false sun reigns supreme, never going down
as she smiles down like a benevolent capitalist…

I long for home, to hug the heat of our nights
and see the moon, somewhere, hanging in the sky.
I become Odysseus, a warrior seeking Sirius.

II
They are not everyday experiences,
the loneliness that eats you amid a busy crowd
the distance that takes your mind miles from a room

With organs intact, you lose sight and smell, a mobile statue in a crowd
Medusa's minion, you wonder if your Penelope would wait…
and loneliness gives birth to the void, Chaos reborn

You fill the void with what work you can,
you seek them in curves – of flesh or of glasses
or look for butts – of cigarettes or other kinds

You burrow into graver sins that expand your hole
and become pain relievers, healing the second
an investment in more potent sorrows on growing tomorrows

You tick time in a million more sins/write as if to Telemachus/
take long walks down Brighton's beach
till dusk's depression and dawn/Apate will hug you again.

The vanity of the scholar's dream
(On a Brighton night, after hearing of a Nigerian student's suicide)

I

The window shows me
A thick fog. I look closer
And see a dead dog.

II

No one will tell you a man died here
Decked in the glory of a mighty home
Laurels in a truckload
This is where blood spills.

It is the hanging axe at your neck
Pushing you to breathe a lie
This is where your voice leaves
This is where your man dies.

III

Starlit Brighton night,
Save me from my thousand fears
Save me from the tears of an evil son
A clouded soul with a cloak too thick.

I fall asleep on many nights to a vision
Mother spits blessings into the River Benue
River Mother, River, this is for the child of my broken waters,
You must protect him, Mother River
River that saved us from invaders as we left Swem hills
While riding on ikyarem the snake. We are saved of the water
No water shall defeat us.

Aôndo moulds her words into favour and peace calls
But the damnation of dollars pound, then become a chained stone to my

heels

The sea beckons from my window in Brighton's Marina
But I drown the sounds in work
Then women, drinks and events
Grasping for glory as the last straw
Gasping for life while loneliness hugs me close
Calling me to go to the sea again and become one with it.

Mother's prayers call from across the river and I struggle
While the sea sings sonorous songs, inviting me
To be a witness to its dark bed…

IV
On this dead winter night,
A scholar writes his soul away
Crashing to a thousand sins of the damned
Lost to cloudless skies, a calling sea
And the loneliness of endless depths.

Incomplete

I throw four pebbles into the sea
As each plops, a ripple forms
Of you and I in a life before
Like this poem...

Converging skies and shadows

We walked down a dried riverbed,
our laughter echoed the emptiness of sand.
Suddenly, the skies converged, you found your feet.

The clouds covered the morning
rains swallowed the grounds
and from all corners, washed every footprint that was us.

II
Your memory is dead at the riverbanks.
The winds compete, but silence holds my hand
and drags my weary feet to despair.

At the final plunge of day,
darkness stretches an invitation:
Macbeth's dagger points to my heart.

A ritual of flames and silence

(for Joan Jonathan and many others who winked in the dark)

There's a ritual of flames atop candles
red caps swaying, casting shadows on walls
whose heights decrease
lives whispered away to eternities of silence—
       or hopeful peace—
where the reaper harvests hopes,
taking souls to gates where answers put stops
to upturned sickles that rule time

There's a carnival of walking corpses
carrying crosses few people note.
As we say *hi*-s and *byes,* dropping notes of forgetting,
the birds chirrup to the tick of time.

Perdition and grace

Depression is a shy bull seeking islands where marooned souls escape to eat of
    deep-seated sorrows hidden in smiles, broad laughs and distant looks.
Depression rides my soul, creates unease, then draws me to waters to calm the
    wilderness of your loss.

I seek grace:
Is living without loving not perdition, Love?

I answer the call of lost souls, walking on in the drought of your presence that
    draws me to River Benue's bed, where many have slept to damnation.

Hemingway, Plath, Sexton, Sello Duiker and Berryman inspire alternate routes

We must travel in the direction of our fears
Or must we?

II
Now I stand at the banks, watching dusk kiss filled lands in spaces
Your memory is a spirit of the earlier unease that keeps me company in
    sounds that echo silence.
I tie a million regrets to my back and get ready to make my plunge to these
    beds where hugged pains would be forgotten
A final thought comes in—are we simply the blink of a dying deity?
I ask for a sign to keep me alive, then the skies open in rains.

Walking on the Spirit of thoughts

I am walking on water
A spirit floating in the heart
Of mist
The thought is stronger than matter
The waves lengthening the thread
Of what lies within

The eyes tell of what the brain thinks
Legs on land while the spirit sees something else
That which the vision fixes
If the owl would lose the night-sight to dawn
Maybe the glasses would fall
To reveal more brightness than the evil
Drawn by a cloak that belittles dreams

But I am walking on water
A spirit floating in the heart
Of mist
And if eyes betray brains, I am not
Betrayed. I will walk on
My thoughts stronger than the matter
Of sight.

The cloak of this present darkness

Show me this darkness, Lord
Eating the light of my eyes
Bring the soul of sound,
Bouncing off these struggles that deafen my sanity

The waters before me wave to the lashing rains
The thunders clap the drums and the skies snap shots
Yet, this darkness hides a mystery
Locked in the kernel of my soul

Beyond, the million lights of neon monsters rush past:
Metals carrying crazier robots who stir their destiny
On lanes moving back and forth
In dizzying motions to the edge of reason
Lost in the pursuit of our borrowed illusion
Of the light at the end of our endless tunnels.

My heart carries a different note
Of scars, breasts and lost affections
Shared like the waters to all
  Who come to view pleasures and glittering waters in the day
  Who find here now, dark clouds hovering over angry waves
Building up and calling:
Come to me all you who labour
And are heavy-laden, and I will give you rest…

I hear the voice of this darkness singing an invitation
I look into its depth and only see shadows
Stretching for a hug

Shadows are my reality, and I fear
This darkness has become too stark.

The cloak of the harmattan priest

The texture of my belief finds strength
in feelings you stole from the winds
powered across rivers and oceans
that gathered in my heart

I breathe through time's nostrils
past passions packed in unmoved seasons

I am moved to beliefs
as I hold to heart, yet again
what remains of absence
and the things left to memory.

On a silvery moon

The silver lady shows several sides
Losing weight as she becomes a banana
Swelling slowly till she fills up to a brilliant calabash
Silver patches illuminating far lands
Smiling to little flies who carry lamps twinkling
Every night borrowing solar glory trapped which the sun's harshness hides

She tames her golden lover and traps off his streaks
When she covers a sack over his glory and heat
Forming a circle around her glow, sprinkling light to farthest ends
Dots rise slowly around, the Almighty's point of little candles

And in every dark sky, you can find light
No matter the spread, dots of grace join
Hidden sometimes by clouds but alive, every night.

TO THE DARK NIGHT

I raise a haiku
the night swallows her glow
nothing makes sense now.

Darkness becomes the night

I looked to the skies
where mud danced in puddles

I matched carefully with the others
the stars trampled under our burning feet

as the night withered slowly, we raised our worries
answered by demons above who blessed us with dead candles.

The stars are orphans tonight

(for the F. G. C Yauri and Chibok girls)

The stars are orphans tonight
Dim dots in the skies hanging to the pluck
Their eyes open to the plight
Of a slow march of drowning souls
Winds whispering weeping wails

Mud shines in the hearts
Of men whose balls swing as their pendulums
Beat time, forcing their way through sealed paths
Their panting sighs bring cries
Laughs crowning beasts accursed in deepening thrusts

Faster… Faster… Faster…

Rods are poked deeper again into torn midpoints
Blood gushing as hands go limp, never aspiring to stretch
Beyond raped ambitions
Closing shutters behold animal glints
Of pigs with beards grunting
To the tears of angels whose wings are torn

Little dots peep out, hidden candles
Put off as the night covers her face
While winds whisper weeping wails…

Muted moos in their moans
(a poem on the Tiv, Benue, Plateau and Taraba killings)

Cows trample fields, mooing to the cackle of gunfire herders spray
like pesticides on villages harvesting heads as they milk skulls for blood

Muted moos in their moans, farmers become animals
Eternally stung by a silence—
      [...
        of destinies punctuated to a stop by herding shots and swords
        of memories hanging in huts where love once reigned
        of security lords who watch from towers, stuffing ears with hate
        of government watching from the stands how history is written in
           bullet wounds
        of a nation sighing to the dying wails of an endangered tribe
        ...]
—   that spreads a poison that drowns a unity of aged love.

     II
Accursed, the people look to *arsehole* rock,
smelling its putrid fart, they look
                    d
                       o
                            w
                                 n
                                      into their hearts
and roll their sorrows on faith's beads
seeking grace as the night swallows them all.

Losing a flower

Nabillah Usman's [@TheNabilahusman] tweet:
*Daily Trust reports that 13 girls of FGC Yauri have been married off to
their abductors. These children were taken from their homes 8 months ago. 3
others who were released in January returned home pregnant. To have your
body stolen from you in this manner is gut-wrenching*

[This is the story of an individual, several individuals. This is also the
story of our states and our nation, kidnapped, raped, and destroyed.]

I

There are words she probably would say, which you would call cliché
this young flower thinned into a soft thorn,
her body stolen
several times in eight months. First, from school where spitting fire
floored educators and mates, while colleagues were carted off like goods in a
    warehouse.

II

Evelyn watched her mates given off to lions who roam Sambisa, death in the
    wings.

She counted the stars each night wondering if the twinkle of the night was a
    promise
or mockery for the light stolen from them all.
She found hope in the seven sisters, prayed the rosary in their shape
and asked Orion to use his belt to tie back all she had lost.

One night, the clouds covered the skies, and the light was put out.

Their waters doused her innocence as crooked pestles crushed childish bliss in
    thrusts that tore her soul.
Rough hands clasped the cries from her mouth after several slaps.
The animals grinded their grunts in toast to Eros, praising Allah for the gift

of renewal; flesh and virgins who they devour in this life, for heaven is too
far.

III

There are words she probably would say, which you would call cliché
this young flower thinned into a soft thorn,
her body stolen
several times in eight months. First, from school where spitting fire
floored educators and mates, while colleagues were carted off like goods in a
    warehouse.
[…]
As she returns home, hollow-eyed, spiral ribbed with a bud in her belly,
we wonder what this new life will breed.

close your eyes for a second

close your eyes for a second
hear harmattan winds howl
it is the sound of several children
shouting silently from mounting despair

their voices echo in the pain of silence
from others who live that they might die
starving while several scribbles define charters
without action that seal their sustainable demise.

hope holds hands

hope holds hands shutting screaming sounds
it hides the emptiness of a paunch and
sharp arched bones protecting rotting insides

hope puts fire into lanky limbs
that claw against the earth
fighting

for food ferried away in exchange for a future
knocking at barred doors and…
a silence that slaps the heart

Nightmares raised on the fringes of pain where the vulture becomes our emblem

On the fringes of nightmares, we endure pain
Holding dreams where
      greens replace black fields
      harvests of grains displace gold and clear waters
      flow through lands in every place
      where soot loses hold of the air

In our nightmares, lived through dawning dusks
      Existence is governed by devils that tune evil
      Owls hoot trumpets that resound doom
      Bullets refine the state of our union
      Bunkers are permanent holdings
      Grenades the *shot put* used to pursue glory

Leagues of fallen angels assemble at plants
To surprise suited apes dressed in colonial robes
As rigs fall, crashing on the back of the giant eagle
      Whose wings are plucked by depleting barrels
      Whose weights lose value with a dropping dollar

Marshlands send signals to Northern cabals
Fights for cultural heirlooms are
      restarted on sensible and senseless plains
In the name of brazen gods and dying men
Poverty, hunger and sicknesses become arsenals that fuel
Freedom fighters, crusaders and jihadists
Daughters and mothers *back* bombs strapped in place of kids
Ladles are replaced with Uzis, AK47s, Danes and SMGs

In the ashes of fallen fathers
Twenty children rise, waiting to be dropped
By shots that should have saved them

Martyrs robed as rebels by powers that be
In the Arsehole Rock

We welcome the herald of a new Christ
Singing *Hosanna* — and others say Baba! —
At this second coming
Long denied by vultures and bats
Wizards and witches riding on umbrellas
Who swiftly change their ships to brooms

We welcome our messiah to clean these Augean stables
The Niger and Benue available to flush out all filth

Baba flies with our killers on his broom,
Stays a second, then flies away
To the crossed dome of British holdings
Reality turns its face:
Our horses lose their strength,
Our eagle loses its flight — or is that a raven?
The vulture is our national emblem.

On the fringes of our nightmares, we endure pain
Holding depleting dreams where
      greens replace black fields
      harvests of grains displace gold and clear waters
      flow through lands in every place
      where soot loses hold of the air

Dreamscapes

I've painted pictures
across several dreamscapes
seeking faces to a fertile future
as sands dropped rapidly down the glass

somewhere, in a maze of infinite obscurities
time uncloaked age, a slow flare of the soul's rage.

The Waiter of the Skull

(Nigeria, Ukraine, Russia, and beyond…in different contexts leading to one end)

vultures circle in
smiling
all around, hyenas cackle
prowling where men once stood

silence is a companion that holds everyone close
peace for the muted fallen
muteness for the souls dying alive
in the noise that becomes the waiter's song

bombs are the firecrackers
celebrating pieces
blown for breakfast
bullets riddle bodies for lunch
dinner a potpourri of disaster none can say
hunger is served as the meal in-between
grief the plate on which these are served

death is the waiter
serving drinks drawn from veins
vinegar on hyssops
for the saved and despised
everyone sips, slowly
fear the stick taking it to the lips

will they be remembered in paradise tonight?

Mbalom, Benue and the lambs

(for Fr. Felix Tyolaha, Fr. Joseph Gor, Mbalom and Naka)

On a quiet dawn in Mbalom,
two priests and a congregation
become lambs slain on St. Ignatius's altar
as camouflaged herders march through town.

Elsewhere, memory raises the pain of the transgressions
of suspicious herders turning River Benue's waters to rich crimson.

Smokes accompany wails as pictures showed many ends:
    old souls sprawled in double pools of red and brown
    shit and excreta dancing for attention with bullet-designed bodies...
    roasted meat fills the air, a cannibal delight as charred flesh litter town
    ...and a suckling baby begins to lick the blood that slowly drips from her
        mother's head
    elsewhere, a child crawls from a bunker that is his father's bulleted body
    ...and becomes a million scattered pieces shattered by a bomb.

there's no hiding place down here
(for the souls trapped beneath the mountains of the Benue and Plateau)

oh, there's no hiding place down here… no, there's no hiding place down here,
oh I went to the rock to hide my face, rock cried out: no hiding place
there's no hiding place down here…down here… down here…

angelus bells are a foretelling to flee from one zone
as muezzins warn: to be there is a dare

flee! flee! flee! catch on to the winds
run and let your wings soar: fly!

but the clouds are a collection of arrows that fall
and the mountains will hide no more as the hills echo our sorrow

ayem o, ayem o, ayem o, ayem o…
oh! oh a oh!

mom de kwagh u ayem o…
I've stopped this running o…

so, we sit and look…changing spaces
holding on to our memories

living, looking, and picking
what parts we can

forgetting yesterday was another BOMB
yesterday was another youth clash of forty dead

of cattle trampling on our fields
of herdsmen silencing our sons

forgetting parts or whole bodies lost in explosions

attending funerals where frogs are buried in empty caskets

the media counts our loss
as a summary of a hundred victims –

numbers without a name thrown whose memories we drown
in a recession of violence covered in a mass grave

we gather our souls to the mountains
but its stones slowly fall on us

the mountain shouts:
there's no hiding place down here!

we leave the mountains and force our lives
on, making new realities that defy our times

my father goes to work
smiling, waving

we wave back and play away with empty bullet cases—
toys no one bothers 'bout any more

the sun sinks
and we desert care as we wear frowns

wondering where time has kept father…
we search the anthills, hives and snake holes

behind a cloud approaching dawn, we find our father on a pole
a head without a body

decapitated by swords that could have been kin's
maggots already coming from his skin

open eyes, with an open mouth
mocking the beauty that we once were

we look to the mountains and frown
weighed from carrying our cross

the mountains look down
mocking our loss

somewhere, the muezzin calls again to the faithful
angelus bells are a foretelling: to live is…to die

The muezzin call and angelus bells

> *Anything worth thinking about is worth singing about.*
> - Bob Dylan

I wake to the muezzin's call
But the loudspeaker does not call to their faithful
The speaker calls to the faithless
To desert the worship of soft cushions and beds.

Inhale.

The cold slaps away any comfort
And there's no fire in sight
So, I knock several thoughts together –
      You, here.
      You, there.
      Us, in between.
It sparks a fire that warms in to out.

Exhale.

It is time to worship
At the feet of flaming thoughts
I see blood robed bodies
Voices pleading for mercy
While the faithful sing senseless songs
Weapons held high and descending

Ascending   Descending
Descending   Ascending

Rivers flow of cut journeys
And leaving wholes, split in a million mutilations.

Inhale

I wait for the angelus bells to ring
It does not remind the faithful to pray
It reminds me of your transition through their swords.

The Almighty looks at me, frowning from his fierce eye in the sky
I shiver, a block in my chest
Taking instructions from the deep

I curse, then drag my mutilated soul out
Lord and tyrant, I will serve
Restless till I stop to witness in the dark.

Exhale.

At the IDP camp

Rain drops trickle down faces
Each drop is a memory of pain

People look with bleak balls staring out of sockets.
Home is a fire they long for as they gather under canopies,
waiting for food that hardly comes.

Children play. Oblivious.

We are flushed into camps
(*IDPs – fancy term for Internally Demonized People*)
We gather like sheep in stalls, beasts on display
photo-op for the evening news.

Déjà vu, a commentator whispers somewhere.

As we gather the sadness of our hearts, mourning losses,
we await tomorrow's pain served with a new helping of rain
and an ever-renewed sorrow.

Haiku 12

The stars are shining,
even as rains keep pouring,
leaving us all drenched.

DREAMSCAPES, NIGHTMARES & DARKNESS

On our dreamscapes, we behold nightmares
Where the vulture becomes our emblem
A foretelling of no hiding place when the muezzin calls.

The crickets chirp, and we weep this dusk
No moon in the sky but minutes give birth to eternal declarations
As another battle rages for our souls.

A foretelling

The worst fear is of a death foretold

Watching flesh squeeze out
Ribs spread out
A case on sheets
Looking with empty sockets

Each morning is a journey of fingers
Down chaplet beads
Invoking lost saints
Quaking hearts shaking
In hope's despair

A death foretold –

.

A full stop before the first letter of a sentence

No moon in the sky might need conversion

We were there, three of us poets smoking our sorrows
The two of them melted into one as their shared sins met
I was a stranger, an island surrounded by their flowing pains
Pushing away gathering pricks from forces without, counting clouds
That came together fighting the eternal diamonds across the sky's blanket

They shared bottles of hurt and sipped slowly of their burdens
Looking straight into a night where past shadows lay hidden
the magnet of their worries held me there, a loner seeking peace, they
Who soon forgot me as they merged, clothes peeled off to mergers
Of intimacies that cemented kinship beyond pain, satisfying lusts
Igniting animals the world pulled mixed faces at in turns

I watched on, swallowing the knowledge of wrong decisions
That dawn would throw a blanket over
One where parties would walk to a forever after
Another memory added of troubles that might never end
As minutes give birth to eternal declarations.

When minutes give birth to eternal declarations
(after the polls and sentiments of a tenure)

I behold her as she looks to me
Somewhere, Eden screams with fire
She strokes my pipe for water:
This fireman shall rise to the quest

Her painful breasts and I write a poem
Where I have no rest but thoughts of the onion bulbs
Slowly rubbing off against the linen that is her shirt
I take lips to kiss the cheeks like the Master
A pained sigh escapes, and my tongue transfers loyalties
Refusing to sell greater passions for thirty pieces
Of hurt that will kill higher desires

We rock away without reason
Senses locked to midlands where thrusts
Answer lusts that keep pounding

Finally, two animals are released, then calmed
Quenched sensations restoring senses
That declare divorces morning will cement

To kill the sun and steal the moon

Some people will shoot the sun to still the moon.
They will romance night
shut shutters
and forget the beauty of daylight

Later, in the moon's hold
they will seek the feel
of the glaring King of the sky

Too late, frost will teach
sometimes romance is a lie.
They will sigh, they will cry
and watch their joys fly.

Another battle for body and soul

First, the soreness seizes the throat and clear speech ceases
You clutch to the huskiness that escapes your lips
As you defy pain to rap with an accent into your phone

The girls melt at first, the girls they do
        Your voice has never sounded this cool…
You take your words in slow, invented baritone
Cough does not collaborate enough to let them
Remain liquid; you rasp some chokes
They sympathise, then leave

Your nose starts a race,
*Bolt*ing faster than your legs that turn to lead
The ailment becomes Medusa and forces you to a bed
A million drugs and increasing irritations later, you find
That a forgotten toothache still exists

Sleep becomes a stranger
Night becomes stark and long forked
Stretching to an expanse of thirty-six hours
You keep the watch, counting sheep
Combing memories while fevers fry you

Lastly, dawn shall come with its fierce face.

Full cycle

It is the travails of our lives
Heaped one on the other, like a storm
That shake our foundations to the core

But these cockroaches survive.
Two out of them take our place
In this world where Noah is forgotten.
Spermified, the ootheca soon carries a million eggs
Planted in places where our memory should be
Moistening it with care we refused to give.

Once your mind is set on a dream,
Everything becomes a clue.

When the full cycle comes once more
And wings guide us to the skies
As we seek to make sense of a senseless destruction
That doesn't remember we ever were
Maybe then…
      Maybe one day, we shall be born again.

MESSIAHS

we seek the lord
like a dog trying to catch its tail
always finding ourselves at the beginning
of an end that makes past evils seem a miracle
while we wait, biding time to clock four more chimes
waiting once more for messiahs who stay within or growing
wolves who mourn with us as we watch tetrarchs bore away our whole.

the road home

these roads
      are a collection
            of fine gravel
hiding miseries and sweat
blood mixed with tar poured to be trampled upon
by common and upper wheels

these roads
      are not the sum
            of our souls
you can glimpse them in the holes
we deliberately dig, bouncing to life's several bumps
in wide expanses of curses flung around

these roads
      lead home
            but
      home is
        where we serve the tale of our souls
buried in the laughter
of those whose lives are the end of our journey

home

home is where the heart… *hiss*

home is living memory
a small pile of shit
waiting
to
hug your eyes
tickle your nose
(and) kiss your feet

it is the sight of plain bums
squatting at weird angles
saluting flies who kiss the holes
dropping prospective maggots
as more legs come to squat
and spread *nyamanyama*
where our pride should be

but beyond stiff one-sided narratives
knock

the door opens and home becomes a tease
where we *kerewa* passions *singing* in frenzied harmony
a radio blares showkey and others *galala* away their frustrations
later, a *kaakaki* blends to drums and we *swange* our hips

home turns to bars where barks without bites resonate
as smiles cover our hearts' miles in sweats, we adjust slowly
and our suffering becomes a lesser burden tuning to Fela's beats

home is where our hearts…ease

Futile butts

(after Aôndosoo Andrew Labe, a verse for our leaders, after the marriage feast)

Flies time the hole and converge in numbers
like planes easing to the tarmac
touching down to dance on the displayed...

There were dry patches of shit
clinging to his bare buttocks
like eczema to skin
the prospective mother-in-law smiled
it was the price for the bride
a homage to sell his shame
       to *buy* her hand...

They waited some more, drinking as the clan laughed
pouring libations to ancestors who frowned

and the flies pay homage

      Time flies, and our man
      has a fight with our woman
      a knife slashes the rope that once bound both hearts
      she packs the folds of her life together, then leaves
      and a solemnisation ticking on a calendar days away
      is made futile

      His drugged steps swept the earth—
      one heavy drag, weary with regret, after another
      each a memory of pain birthed in former joys
      disgrace drowned and love proclaimed
the road seemed far, but each step dragged his weary soul
to her home

no butt show shall be made futile
and he makes a demand
that they return back their stares
or put Humpty back
    to patch his shattered soul

Tenderness and presence {Three Poems}

I. They are there
the fires that fry us
are lit by friendly demons
who quench it once in a while
to let the smoke squeeze our chest
and let the waters flow from our eyes

they are there
hands exchanging notes
ensuring paint is poured over stones
that slowly disintegrate to have worse liquid—

our blood
and more grain for their roads
formed from our broken skulls and limbs

they are there—
        who collect a thousand bills
for pills, then convert them to meal tickets
that fatten their bloated brethren as we go to hospitals
where we beg injections or seek drugs
       ~~to end our damnation~~
       for mercy killings rather than wait
to be chewed by this prolonged cancer
gnawing at us and spitting our spirits
to depths where memory cannot hold

the fires burn our entirety
frying the fibres of our every thread
and
    once
       in a very long while

the fires are put out by friendly demons
who blow us kisses…

then we get choked again
in the smoke they spread
before they rekindle the fires again
to their gain.

II. Tenderness survives
the tenderness survives
beneath the carnage put in place
to rape your mind of its innocence

the tenderness survives…
       to put the angst in your brain
to put the anger in your hands
to be poured on that young man
       who takes a loaf of bread
that man
       caught
       mobbed
       … roasted…

the angst is poured to power your limbs
to strip the girl
       who steals a phone to sell to save her soul
the girl on whose chest
       your hands rain blows
       your feet rocket kicks
as ready hands lustily pull off her pants…

for them all, many phone clicks
       fly to twitter, spiralling into blogs
       viralling the shame of a misdirected hate
       that breaks our humanity

yet…

III. An endless love for the lords of the band
the sirens usher their presence
we hail them, lords of the band
who bloat on our blood
suffering ulcers from too much
fats…
    scraped off our bones

we blow kisses to these 'saviours'
who deliver us from a life of bliss

the tenderness comes off
as another one of us falls

at the graveside of our own
we shout ourselves hoarse
swearing at our loves, the lords
brewing storms in calabashes
full of palm wine and *burukutu*
that we take to our lips
as we promise to avenge the ones silent…
even as we return to our shacks
where flies kiss our open sores

then

the sirens sound again
we rush from our gutters
and clean up to impress our lords
we pour our garments on the ground:
    hosanna! hosanna!

and lay our backs up on the road
to fill the potholes they have ignored

let their tyres crush our souls

the tenderness persists
in our love for our lords
and we hail them again:
precious loves, lords of the band

The two sides of a step

We fetch silence from wells of sorrow
Deep, dug by keepers who herd
Wolves in cow clothing
Thrown among us

They
    Have
        Built
           Steps
              Towards
                    Our
                        Death
                    And
                We
           Descend
       Slowly

We let go of the *guga*
As we dive to depths
Forgetting the steps

And a million wolves eat our entrails
from within…

The dreams shall find you

> *Amongst other experiences, suspected herdsmen attacked and opened fire*
> *on a congregation during morning Mass in Mbalom, instantly killing the*
> *priest and the congregants.*

they are there tonight
the ones pressed against their will
and those whose songs you drowned in the benue

they shall   —   wait in your dreams
        —   your orchids shall become maggots
        —   and your sun shall die before you rise

hell shall not wait but find you
as you try to throw a blanket over lost memory
before you get to eternity's gates

satan impatiently awaits with the fork
hoping to bless you, cursed runt, who sentenced
our loves to a night that came when their sun was rising

The three sides of confinement
(in memory of Mandela and all of us)

a weight steals the soul
a heart loses its beat and runs wild
as thoughts crisscross its orbit like lost stars.

memories are lava melting in the heat of my heart
as images remain within me, like souls trapped in a frame.

collected waste whiffs into this room
my first mate in this confinement—
rats— run along and force me to run, too,
into ghosts & memories… soon, we all become friends.

outside is forever away and an agony
i long for nothing as i try to paint tales out of darkness
and bleak ceilings using the only light channelled to this hole,
a crack in the wall that ushers in roaches who crawl in to salute my presence.

time's spirit is lost as my friends become my meals
i bloat on ghosts and memories, rats and roaches
and i lose all that once was me.

II
seconds tick into months of endless oblivion
that leave me lost in the folds of falsehoods

i lick the lie of what lies trapped
and spit its sourness, easing away soreness
finally, forgiveness frees foes time uncloaks to be me.

The Owner of All

If you bet with me in the name of spirits
I will play the flute with my load on my head

Who belongs to all belongs to none
But he who really owns us all

As rivers flow with their many troubles
So will we pass through with the currents

Weave then a path to the end
Hugging spiders who will give you silk

Dawn never sees the face of those beloved for
Aôndo does not leave his child tied overnight

These dots of history will find eyes
And crosses where an after ascension will breed grace.

SEQUENCE TO FINAL FLOWS

Thundering drums and cannons call afar from Idoto
answer softly from your end, life calls us to a dance.

For the sequence between metamorphosis
keep your verse for our hearts, understand the sun
and build a bridge for birds.
Enjoy a thousand sparkles, then set sail on a sea of stars.

For the sequence between metamorphosis

Our shaky fingers hold lamps against the wind
at the crossroads to purgatory, awaiting an unveiling
where night unfolds to day and fire becomes the Phoenix again.

Faith sustains dying lights to keep the hearth warm
beyond the night when bleak sorrow drapes a blanket
over the stars.

Amid chaos, this is the wait,
sequence between metamorphosis

Caterpillar, hold the door open for your butterfly:
    Night, let the hours tick slowly till the cock cries
    Dawn – create a rhythm for fluttering eyes
    Dusk – trap some rays as the sun dives below earth's belt
    Night, tide us slowly on to dawn while we wait.
Caterpillar, hold the door open for your butterfly.

Keep your verse for our hearts

(for my siblings: Sharamang, Saddiq, Sibbyl, Daisy, Debbie, Oko, Romeo & David)

Sometimes the ingredient for fine verse
        – is a trip into the recesses of the mind
        dredging demons from (blurred) past and present problems
        – is a broken heart and a longing for bottles
        cigars, metals or just a rope to end the misery
        – are rants and posing in public spheres, trading lives
        for likes and shares, with no love to go home to.

Your verse is music, and in my mind, a formula appears:
(Mis)Fortune + ♮ + Silence | Chaos = Notes + Music + (Dis)Quiet x Ink of your
thoughts = Verse
We dig deep into the soulful equation, shut eyes, smell grace
        & drink of your essence.

We find our freedom in expressions, laced through verse
therein lies hope, something beautiful.
If we | you listen,
        it is a promised unveiling
like night unfolds to day; like the caterpillar to a butterfly.

Flee from Plath's path, tender soul and only let the oven bake testimonies
mash your ashes with verse, and let sadness become the vine
wine to our buds as you spit the angst of rage, loneliness and silence.

Faith sustains the dying lights to keep the hearth warm
beyond the night when bleak sorrow drapes a blanket
over the stars.

Rise, Phoenix, your fire forges wings,
fly now beyond despair to heaven's peak.

If the sun wasn't so mean

(inspired by Margaret Ifeoma Osuji, for us all)

If the sun wasn't so mean,
you would not know the beauty of the moon's grin.
If the day wasn't so harshly bright,
you would not consider the soothing of the night.

Death stretches out to capture our pearls
to teach the adage forever sells,
that you value what you have,
in the finite space blessed by the one who did us all carve.

The sun is mean if you miss its grin,
the day is harshly bright if you forget its light,
wonders and continuous wonders,
that transcend the confines of our mere thoughts.

Life's lesson is best captured in its strife,
its beauty in the emptiness of its duty
to death, a deferent departure from this earth,
dawn's fullness through a day till dusk and then morn.

If the sun wasn't so mean, dear,
there would be much to fear
a deathly chill — need I say the rest?
Enjoy the sun — it hurts but know through it, we are blessed.

Bridge for birds

Build me a bridge for birds
                    flying forth
in wings carrying truth
the wind blessed carrier
charting the course
for the oceans blessing their cross
our ornate hearts leaping towards
shapes formed heavenwards

Simple hopes, ropes
with which we are hanged, banged
by the mistrust paid for by those who promises made

Bless the Benue, our love cries
a collective voice rises
changing down to up, centring a top
for these new ones, who this once
carry our burdens
feathers singly plucked by congruent sins
for humans they be
the small bridge to see
and cross
not to drown…

Build us all now
a bridge before we fall down
a bridge for birds
unto eternal aerial beds

The thousand sparkles on your stomach

Olukayode asks how the world sinks into the sea
When he sees the sun drawn like a magnet into the waters' bowel
Beyond the farthest holds of our eyes
He looks with wonder when under the harshest smiting of day
We come to offer our troubles to the ease of the waves

We see a thousand snakes in sun-sparkled jewels
Wriggling to the wind's beats as they wave to bystanders from the bridge
The seabed holds histories of lost bones
And the stories of millions whose wings failed in mid-flight and nourished
    the concrete floors in crimson rivers
Or were simply pulled to closure
By mermaids seeking sacrifices of depressed souls
Plunging every season to become seafood

The old seers deliver a different message
Gazing through crystal balls, flipping cowries and seashells
Inscribed, they say, with notes from the deepest parts
Where truth is a mixture of belief and what nonsense books proclaim

The crystal balls witness the advent of stories
The memory of souls who wrestle the dogs at Hades' gates
Fight Poseidon and leap in snaky sparkles wearing jewels stolen
As they rode off on seahorses, gifts for Aôndo or Helios – whoever answers
    first
Praying for a peace that the earth's hold denied them
Seeking to be found worthy of time's embrace

sailing on a sea of stars

(for you, and every one of us)

on this night, i am sailing on a sea of stars
to lands that are far
the moon smiles
and every darkness is forgotten

fires are snuffed to smoke
tales told of all that once was
i shut my soul in flight to the heavens

though the troubles brew strong
i see Aôndo's hands and i know they are long
enough to destroy everything that is wrong

tonight, for one moment
i will forget every torment
raise my voice in song and forget the noise

on this night, i am sailing on a sea of stars
to lands that are far
the moon smiles
and every darkness is forgotten

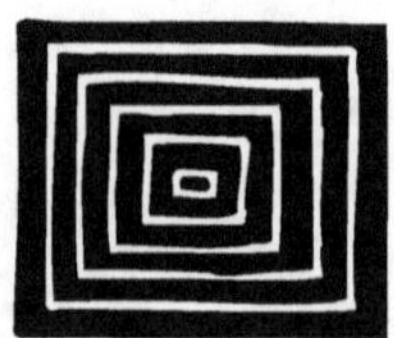

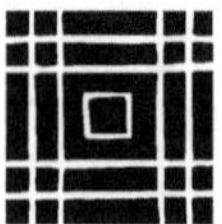

ACKNOWLEDGEMENTS

I am grateful to friends, family and teachers who helped me on the journey to this book. A particular defining event in this season was a workshop in Oxford facilitated by Kwame Dawes, which helped me refocus on discipline, experience and witnessing. I appreciate Niyi Osundare and Hyginus Ekwuazi for many reflections that helped my process. I am grateful to the British Foreign and Commonwealth Office, whose award of a Chevening scholarship in partnership with the University of Sussex enabled me to study in the UK and by extension, to travel more widely.

My wife, Agatha and our daughter, Msen, my Jennifers (Aduro, Emelife, Agbaire), Debbie Iorliam, Tine Agernor, Otene Ogwuche, Oko Owoicho, Torkwase Igbana, Sarah Egbo, Segun Sangowawa, Suraj, Debbie Braide, Gabriel, Theo, Verl, Terhide, Ngohide, Tersoo, Susan Omale, my several cousins from the Adzeges to Shangos, Ayedes and Agemas, Bunmi Fatoba, my Chevening 2018/19 cohort, and many others: thank you for too many things.

Thank you: Servio Gbadamosi, Amara Chimeka, Aondosoo Labe, Romeo Oriogun, Kukogho I. Samson, Daisy Odey, & Deborah Oluniran for literary kinship.

I am grateful to several editors and platforms that helped birth earlier versions of some of the poems here, notably Molara Wood and the Ake Festival magazine for 'Building Memories' and 'The thousand sparkles on your stomach.' Others include 'The Muezzin Call and Angelus Bells' and 'A Song of the Waters' in *Memento* edited by Adedayo A Agarau; 'If Lagos Knew' in *Con-Scio* (Is 1. Vol 3), poetry edited by Jide Badmus; 'A Ritual of Flame & Silence' and 'Building Memories' in *Soro Soke* edited by Jumoke Verissimo and James Yeke; and several poems in the Association of Nigerian Authors annual journal which at some point I published and edited.

I salute literary soldiers and platforms doing very much for the arts across the country at the national stage, including Moses Tsenongu, Chuma Nwokolo, Hadiza El-Rufai, Halima Aliyu, Maria Ajima, Regina Achie-Nege, Efe Paul Azino, Servio Gbadamosi, Adachukwu Onwudiwe, Odoh Diego, Paul Liam, Emman Shehu, Wale Okediran, Lola Shoneyin, Promise Ogochukwu, Jahman Anikulapo, Richard Ali, Umar Sidi, Bash Amuneni, Anselm Ngutsav, Sule Egya, Salamatu Sule, Ahmed Maiwada, Afrika Ocho, Denja Abdullahi, Adedayo Agarau, Uchenna Emelife, B. M. Dzukogi, Dike Chukwumerije, Jerry Adesewo, Kabura Zakama, Charles Iornumbe, Eugenia Abu, Maik Ortsega, Iquo DianaAbasi, Camillus Ukah, Umar Yogiza, and many others. Devoid of any of our faults — and who doesn't have them? — well done! God bless you.

Wherever these lines go, may memory be kind and the waters call only to good.

Su'ur Su'eddie Vershima Agema is a multiple-award-winning writer, cultural activist, and development worker. He is the author of three poetry collections, including *Home Equals Holes: Tale of an Exile* (Winner, Association of Nigerian Authors Prize for Poetry 2014; Nominee, Soyinka Prize for African Literature 2018) and a short story collection, *The Bottom of another Tale* (Shortlisted for the Association of Nigerian Authors' Prize for Prose 2014 and Abubakar Gimba Prize for Short Stories 2015). His story, 'Washing the Earth' won the Mandela Day Short Story Prize 2016, while his poem, 'Tales one shouldn't tell often', was shortlisted for the Saraba/PEN Nigeria Poetry Prize 2013. His 'The Three Sides of Confinement' was shortlisted for the Mandela Day Poetry Prize 2016.

Su'eddie was previously the Black History Month/Project Curator and co-founder/president, African Writers, at the University of Sussex, where he earned an MA in International Education and Development as a Chevening Scholar.

He is currently the Lead Editor and Chief Executive at SEVHAGE Publishers and SEVHAGE Literary and Development Initiative.

Su'eddie blogs at http://sueddie.wordpress.com and http://sevhagereviews.wordpress.com @sueddieagema on Twitter. He lives in a couple of places with his wife, daughter, and members of their clan.